[Incarnation]

Belief Matters

[Incarnation]

The Surprising Overlap
of Heaven & Earth

William H. Willimon

Abingdon Press
Nashville

Incarnation: The Surprising Overlap of Heaven and Earth

Copyright © 2013 by Abingdon Press

All rights reserved.

Library of Congress Cataloging-in-Publication Data

Willimon, William H.
    Incarnation : the surprising overlap of heaven and earth / William H. Willimon.
        pages cm. — (Belief matters)
    Includes bibliographical references and index.
    ISBN 978-1-4267-5754-9 (binding perfect, adhesive, pbk. : alk. paper)
    1. Incarnation. I. Title.
    BT220.W725 2013
    232'.1—dc23

                                                                    2013032724

13 14 15 16 17 18 19 20 21 22—10 9 8 7 6 5 4 3 2 1

MANUFACTURED IN THE UNITED STATES OF AMERICA

To those who demonstrate the Incarnation
through their witness at
Duke Memorial United Methodist Church

Contents

Introduction

We are on our way to a great adventure. We will travel to wonderful, mysterious places you cannot visit on your own, destinations so exotic you must have a guide to lead you there. You will be told secrets that the world does not openly discuss. Your world will be expanded, your life enriched and changed. In the Belief Matters series we will joyfully explore the riches of the faith, the adventure of Christian believing, the gift of Christian theology. We are going to dare to think like Christians. While there is nothing to be gained from overly intellectualizing the faith, there is much to be lost in dumbing down Jesus Christ. For one thing, the church doesn't delight in insoluble cerebral puzzles—life does. As a pastor I discovered that people bring to church bigger, bolder questions than I pose in my sermons. They ask: Why am I unhappy? Is death the last word? Why can't I keep my promises? Is this all there is? If Jesus is the Redeemer, why doesn't the world look more redeemed?

Hucksters, religious and otherwise, prance the Web pronouncing, "Six simple steps to . . ." or, "The secret of happier . . ." The church need not prove the lie behind the allure of simple truth—life does. All around us we see the sad wreckage of those who believed the reductionistic deceit that "it's all just a simple matter of . . ."

More important, Jesus defies simplistic, effortless, undemanding explications. To be sure, Jesus often communicated his truth in simple, homely, direct ways, but his truth was anything but apparent and undemanding in the living. Common people heard Jesus gladly—not all of them, but enough to keep the government nervous—only to find that the simple truth Jesus taught, the life he lived, and the death he died complicated their settled and secure ideas about reality. The Gospels are full of folk who confidently knew what was what—until they met Jesus. Jesus provoked an intellectual crisis in just about everybody. Their response was not, "Wow, I've just seen the Son of God," but rather, "Who is this?"

In this series we explore the riches of Christian believing, wading into deep, faith-engendering waters that provide essential refreshment for disciples. In each book a skilled pastoral theologian will talk about what a doctrine means and why this set of ideas is important for you to think through. The series opens with my invitation to think about the Doctrine of the Incarnation. Hold on to your hats; this may be a wild ride. The Doctrine of the Incarnation makes it possible to say what Christians must say about Jesus Christ. We never needed a Doctrine of Incarnation until we met Jesus—a material, fully human being just like us who was also the eternal unlike us.

Matthew says that when Joseph was told (in a dream) that his fiancée was pregnant—and not by him (God seems to enjoy delivering news like this when we are asleep and defenseless!)—Joseph bolted upright and broke into a cold sweat. Having his world rocked required Joseph to rethink everything he once knew. Joseph could warn us: thinking about the jolt of Incarnation can be a bumpy ride.

Take my hand; we are about to enter deep water. Join my astonishment that Christians don't just believe that Jesus was much like God; we think God is who Jesus is. And because we know that God is like Christ, we know the way the world is moving and what we must do to move with the grain of the universe.

Currently we are experiencing an outbreak of "spirituality." As for me, I pray for a counter resurgence of "incarnationality." In Christ, heaven and earth meet; God gets physical. In seeing Jesus, we believe we have beheld as much of God Almighty as we ever hope to see this side of eternity. "Whoever who has seen me, has seen the Father" (John 14:9), is an astounding statement for anyone to make—particularly if that person is a poor, unemployed, homeless, wandering beggar eventually tortured to death by the government.

On so many occasions Jesus taught us by throwing out a parable beginning with, "The kingdom of heaven is like . . ." He made God's realm mundane by saying, "A woman was kneading dough to make bread" or "A king set out to make war" or "A man had two sons." He revealed heavenly things through earthy, time-bound parables. This inextricable mix of earth and heaven, temporal and eternal, mundane and mysterious characterized everything Jesus did and, so his first followers came to believe, everything Jesus is. We're at the heart of the Christian faith: Almighty God, the same being who hung the heavens and flung the stars in their courses, became a man who lived in Nazareth.

The Doctrine of the Incarnation is thus our human attempt to make sense out of an event that has happened, is still happening—heaven and earth overlapping, interlocking in a Jew from Nazareth who lived briefly and died violently. Then three days later, the women shout, "He's back!" God here. God now.

The Doctrine of the Incarnation is our attempt to think about that.

—Will Willimon

God Revealing God

My first summer of college, bumming around Europe, I sprawled with other students in the middle of the night, near Amsterdam's Dam Square. A student whispered, "Want to see God? Take this." I awoke the next morning at the base of the queen's statue with a bad headache, without a vision of God.

Who doesn't want to see God? Atheists and theists alike are able to read human history as a long search for, and often a wild fantasizing about, God. However, the atheist's, Is there a God? is a less interesting question than the biblical, *Who* is the God who is there? Ninety-five percent of us already believe God is. But there are contentions among us: What does God look like? What does God expect of us?

Does God care about me?

And the most pointed question of all: Does God care about me?

It's fine to ask big questions about us and God. Trouble is, there are reasons having to do with the great gap between who God is and who we are that make it impossible for us, on our own, to give answer. How can creatures accurately conceive of their Creator? Can finite minds grasp the infinite?

Lost in the wilds of Alabama, trying to find my way to a little church, I stopped and asked a man leaning back in his chair before a rural gas station, "How do I get to Bangor?" He scratched his chin, thought a moment, and declared, "Friend, there ain't no way to get there from here."

Thought about God is of the same order—no way to get to God from here. Impressive reasoning, invigorating spiritual experience, devout practices, even deeply religious upbringing, cannot enable us to ascend to God. There's a word for a God who is accessible through our intellectual efforts—*idol.* An idol is a reasonable, believable, conceivable—but alas, fake—god we set up as substitute for the God we are unable to reach from here.

Every religion offers to help us finite creatures climb up to or dig deep into the infinite. Only Christianity contends that the infinite descended, taking the form of our finitude—Incarnation. This book is the good news

> # An idol is a reasonable, believable, conceivable, but fake godlet we set up as substitute for God.

that we need not climb up to God; in Jesus Christ, God comes down to us. I'm using "up" and "down" here figuratively. God is inaccessible to us not only because (as we have traditionally conceived) God reigns in highest heaven and we are down here in the muck and mire of earth. God is inaccessible not only to human sight but also to human reason. Incarnation is the counterintuitive, not-believed-by-nine-out-of-ten-Americans assertion that even though we could not avail ourselves of God, God lovingly became available. God condescended to be God With Us.

> # Incarnation . . . is God condescended to be God with us.

Thinking the Unthinkable

In the first of the Ten Commandments we were forbidden to create any image of God. Counter to much current "spirituality," we are not free to come up with any old "god" who suits our need. In Jesus Christ, it was as if the true and living God said, "Humanity, you want a true image of me? You want the secret of who I really am and what I'm up to? Don't attempt to make an image of me; I'll give you a true icon: Jesus Christ." Jesus Christ is "the image of the invisible God" (Col. 1:15), no less than "the reflection of God's glory and the exact imprint of God's very being" (Heb. 1:3 NRSV).

"Incarnation" (from the Latin word for "in the flesh") is the set of ideas by which Christians believe that Jesus Christ is both divine and human. The Incarnation is the grand crescendo of our reflection upon the mystery that Christ is the full revelation of God—not only one who talks about God but the one who speaks for and acts as God, one who is God. Generally we do not say that God was Christ; more typical for the New Testament is the phrase "God was in Christ" (2 Cor. 5:19 NRSV). Or it is said that the eternal "Word became flesh" (John 1:14).

Not that Jesus Christ—as the visible image of the invisible God—is obviously, self-evidently God. From the first, most people who encountered Jesus said not, "That Jew from Nazareth is God!" but instead, "That's not the way God is supposed to look." A word of warning: most of us have been indoctrinated into the modern, Western conviction that we already have the ability to think clearly about anything. We have all we require

> ## "Incarnation" is the set of ideas by which Christians believe that Jesus Christ is both divine and human.

innately, on our own, to think clearly and truthfully about whatever we choose. Our democratic sensibilities are therefore offended by the thought that the meaning of God is a gift given to some, a phenomenon that we lack the innate skills to comprehend on our own. God must reveal the truth to us or we can't know it.

Why isn't Jesus Christ's divinity more obvious?

Well, for one thing, God is God and we are not. The Old Testament teaches that it is fearful and devastating for mere mortals to gaze directly upon God, as painful as gazing upon the sun. For another thing, we have expectations for how God ought to look and act if God is worthy of our worship. From the first, Jesus failed to measure up to our expectations of God.

> ## From the first, Jesus failed to measure up to our expectations of God.

Danish Christian philosopher Søren Kierkegaard said it would have satisfied our intellectual hankerings if God had appeared as a "very rare and tremendously large green bird" rather than as a homeless rabbi. God surprised us by appearing in human form, as a person who looked suspiciously like the annoying guy next door, an undeniably human person who hungered, thirsted, rejoiced, suffered, raged, wept, and died as all persons do.

And yet, in an astonishingly short time after his death, Jesus' once-disheartened followers began boldly telling the world that when we encounter Jesus, we encounter God. This Jew from Nazareth is as much of the true and living God as we ever hope to see. None of them said, "Jesus lives on in our memories" or "We've had a meaningful religious experience; let us show you how you may have one too." What they said was, "Jesus of Nazareth is the Christ, the Father's Eternal Word, the only begotten Son of God."

This was a shock to probably nine out of ten Near Easterners who assumed that God's primary attributes were unrestrained power and undeniable glory. There's not much power and glory in a crucified rabbi. But those whom the Holy Spirit pushed to greater open-mindedness saw that there was more to God than they previously thought. Once reminded that the main attribute of Israel's God is steadfast, forbearing love, Jesus as Son of God made more sense. If God is not solely power and glory, as we define those things, if God is glorious suffering and powerfully redemptive love, then it made sense that God might indeed come among us as a lowly servant who healed, taught, forgave, suffered, died, and rose to bring us close to God.

> Once reminded that the main attribute of Israel's God is steadfast, forbearing love, Jesus as Son of God made more sense.

How wonderfully ironic that God Almighty should turn out to be most godly precisely in God's suffering and dying for ungrateful, wretched, erring sinners who, by our lives and actions, seemed most distant from holy, righteous God.

The Strangest Story

The only way we know the truth of this God-become-servant is through Scripture, ancient stories that were told by those who were close to Jesus from the first. If we are to know the whole truth about God, we must submit to these ancient writings. The Gospels at times seem a bit like biography, but they are more. In places, they sound like history, but more. They are certainly talking about events that happened at a specific time and place, but they do so in a way that often seems strange. It is a mistake to think that the Gospels sound strange because they are ancient. They are strange because they attempt to describe events that really happened—God coming close to us in Jesus Christ—by events so challenging to our way of thinking that gospel talk sounds odd.

"Luke, tell us what you know to be true about Jesus Christ," and Luke tells a story about a young woman conceiving a child out of wedlock, birthing in a cowshed, sky erupting with angelic proclamations, and, well, you know the Christmas story. Surely Luke would have told us what is true about Jesus Christ in another way if a more acceptable way were adequate for conveying the facts about Christ. Indeed, Matthew, Mark, and John tell remarkably different stories about the advent of Jesus Christ, not to confuse the truth, but rather because the truth they told was both historical and transcendent. Our Gospels describe so much more than mere facts can tell.

Not that the earliest accounts of Jesus are fiction. The Gospels are *not* some sort of primitive attempt at novels. They are realistic attempts to speak about real events in which the witnesses found that their sense of themselves, of their world, and of God got decisively disrupted and rearranged. But what they have seen and heard strains their ability to tell in order to be true to the facts of the matter.

In a sermon preached in 396 CE, Augustine ridiculed a disbelieving world that regards "this stupendous miracle as fiction rather than fact. . . . They despise the human because they cannot believe it; they do not believe the divine because they cannot despise it." Augustine went on to rhapsodize, "The one who holds the world in being lay in a manger; he was simultaneously speechless infant and the Word. The heavens cannot contain him; a woman carried him in her bosom. She was ruling our ruler . . . suckling our bread." A strange wonder evokes strange speaking.

The Scriptures tell us the truth about Jesus, who is in turn the truth about God. If any of us limited creatures is able to comprehend, to believe, and in believing to stake our lives upon the one who was "the way, the truth, and the life" (John 14:6), that believing is also a miraculous work of God among us. Thus we, by the grace of God in our lives, become living testimony of the truth of Incarnation. Theologian Karl Barth said that if you are able to believe in the strange, wondrous birth, your belief is a miracle akin to the miraculous birth of Jesus.

Furthermore, New Testament writers tell these stories and meditate upon the significance of the events they have witnessed not simply to give a detached,

Scriptures tell us the truth about Jesus, who is in turn the truth about God.

disinterested set of facts and figures. They speak as witnesses hoping to convince us that the truth about Jesus Christ is truth for us too. "These things are written so that you may come to believe that Jesus is the Christ, God's Son, and that believing, you will have life in his name" (John 20:31). In telling the story of Jesus, John hopes that we will take our places in the story so that our little stories become part of God's great story called the salvation of the world.

The Gospel account of the wise men and the star or the angels appearing to the shepherds is found only in Luke and Matthew, respectively. We shouldn't be surprised that an earthshaking event should attract to itself all sorts of fanciful legends and wild stories. Perhaps these nativity stories are metaphorical ways of talking about events that were very difficult to describe. But just because we are forced to speak of some strange event in metaphorical ways it does not falsify the reality of the event; in fact it underscores its mind-blowing reality. In an incarnational faith it's okay to think about God using human analogies.

In an incarnational faith it's okay to think about God using human analogies.

I think of the truth of the birth of Jesus through the lens of the birth of our daughter, Harriet. On the day our second child was born, my wife Patsy says that the morning sunlight suddenly flooded in the hospital room and she distinctly heard Cat Stevens singing "Morning Has Broken." For Patsy, this was some sort of strange meeting of the very human act of giving birth with the very divine act of receiving an undeserved, wonderful gift of new life.

Maybe her metaphorical thinking was a window opening onto the true significance of this event. Be well assured that in the birth of our child, something actually happened in our space and time. Whatever happened, there was a surplus of meaning, something more to be learned in the event itself than could be adequately described by the attending obstetrician. The stories of the star, the wise men, the shepherds, the angels singing could have been somewhat akin to what Patsy experienced. The Gospels are proclamations of faith. They are rooted in history, but their intent is clearly more important than to report mere history.

God Coming Close

So-called progressive Christians like John Spong or Marcus Borg, who reject the virginal conception of Jesus or the Resurrection as actual events in time, betray their out-of-hand dismissal of the supernatural. If you grant that God could have created the world out of nothing (which apparently most of us do), then you will also have to grant that God could create a human person apart from human sex. What's important in the belief in the virginal conception of Jesus is not biology or the suspension of it, but rather that God's Son, the Word With Us, came to us through both human and divine agency. Sometimes the church has marveled that God came to us through an unexpected, undeserved divine act, and other times has been stunned that God came to us by being born into an all-too-human family.

Christ, for all of his glory, was "born through a woman" (Gal. 4:4), as you and I were born, as the Nicene Creed puts it, "incarnate of the Holy Spirit and the Virgin Mary." How different would the story be if Christ had descended to us on a cloud from heaven. Jesus had a human mother, bore human genes, carried the imprint of human evolution, and was born to a particular people in a small hick town in Galilee while Caesar Augustus ruled the whole world with an iron fist. Hebrews 2:14-18 says that Christ's full sharing of the human condition is essential to our salvation, a work of a God who amazingly not only created us but also became one of us.

Mormonism's Joseph Smith taught that God was once what we now are and that we can (with help from The Book of Mormon) become what God now is. There is a fundamental continuity between God and the rest of us, a linkage that we can reawaken in ourselves by carefully adhering to The Book of Mormon. When viewed from the perspective of orthodox Christianity, Mormonism sounds suspiciously like first-century gnosticism. Gnosticism presents faith as secret, esoteric wisdom that only a few enlightened souls can attain. Each of us is born with a divine spark. By cultivating the divine within ourselves, by inculcating special secret knowledge (Greek, *gnosis* = knowledge) we can ascend to our original divine state. Thus Mormonism tends to speak of Jesus as a revealer of God, whereas orthodox Christianity views Christ as our reconciler to God.

The Christian faith teaches that we do not get over our estrangement from God by acquiring spiritual knowledge or philosophical insight; only God, through an act of God, can solve the problem between us and God. That's one reason Christianity has always taught that the world was created by God from nothing. God is neither dependent upon the world nor a creation of the world; the world is dependent upon God. God is not material or time-bound; we are.

However, in the Incarnation, God (as Gregory of Nazianzus put it) "remained what he was and took up what he was not." God became human without diminishment of God's divinity; God's divinity thoroughly embraced our humanity. Thus our reconciliation to God is effected not by something we do (as in Mormonism's theology of human ascent) but by something that God has done and continues to do in Jesus Christ (God's gracious descent).

> In the Incarnation . . . God became human without diminishment of God's divinity; God's divinity thoroughly embraced our humanity.

The miracle of the birth of Jesus, maintained from the earliest church and confessed in its creeds, is, in theologian Karl Barth's words, not cause for intellectual debate but rather a "summons to reverence and worship." Barth charges that the narrow-minded thinking of those who deny the creed's "born of the virgin Mary" are in the last resort to be understood only as stemming from a desire for an all too near or all too far-off God.[1]

Fully Divine, Fully Human

Please don't think that our utter dependence upon ancient scripture puts you at a disadvantage in thinking about Immanuel, God With Us. Again, Kierkegaard imagined a contemporary of Jesus who, in order to uncover the real truth about Jesus, hired secret agents who spied upon Jesus and kept exact eyewitness accounts of his every word and move. Alas, they were forced to report that Jesus was "an unimpressive man of humble birth, and only a few individuals believed there was anything extraordinary about him."[2]

The true significance of Jesus was hidden from many who were in closest proximity to him. He often confused his own mother. He constantly befuddled the same disciples he presumed to teach. In the end, Jesus dies seemingly abandoned by his Father. His miracles were dismissed as the tricks of any wandering, wonder-worker.

The Doctrine of the Incarnation, God's enfleshment in Jesus Christ, is the church's attempt to think clearly about the great mystery that Matthew introduces as a child named "Jesus, because he will save his people from their sins" (Matt. 1:21); Mark depicts as a wonder-working, crucified stranger; and Luke says was conceived of the Holy Spirit impregnating a virgin named Mary.

"God is not a human being" (Num. 23:19 NRSV) is an undisputed, consistent scriptural truism. The vast majority of Americans already believe that God is eternal, immortal, invisible, omnipresent, omniscient, and a stack of other high-sounding, ethereal abstractions, the antithesis of everything human, or so we thought.

Until we met Jesus.

No one disputed that Jesus was not a real man. As a Jewish man, he said and did things that most humans do. Nobody doubted that Jesus had a body. He spit in the dirt. He bled and hurt like hell on the cross. After a full day on the road, he was tired and had to get away for rest and prayer. He got angry, especially with people who presumed they were tight with God. On a couple of occasions, he broke down and wept. In every way, except sin, Jesus fully shared our humanity.

No one disputed that Jesus was not a real man.

But he also said and did things—forgiving sins, performing miraculous signs and wonders, authoritatively speaking for God—that nobody but God can do. Jesus appeared to be so godlike, so at one with God, that he not only spoke in an easy and intimate way of God as "Father," but also quite early on his followers spoke of him as "Son of God."

After his resurrection, his divinity seemed self-evident to those who worshipped him and experienced his presence. Yet even in his resurrection, even in his freedom from many of the limitations that bind us, Jesus still had a kind of body, still ate breakfast with his disciples on the beach and broke bread at suppertime, still spoke to them.

Jesus was no disembodied spirit fluttering above human life. Clearly he cared about real people who were caught in real, earthly, human binds—babies to be birthed, children to be raised, bills to be paid, and an upper room to be prepared. He gathered disciples and embraced the hungry multitudes. He healed the sick, cast out demons, and invited ordinary folk to walk with him. When he noted hunger, he offered bread. When the wine ran out, he made more. Rather than providing people an escape route out of this world, he intruded into the full, tragic human condition, modeling a new way of living in this world. You can almost taste the dust as he walks along Galilee's roads. The Gospels speak of him not in the fashion of a "Once upon a time in a faraway land," but rather by locating him in real time, such as "during the reign of Caesar Augustus," and in real places like Bethlehem and Golgotha. He not only brought a message that was addressed to real people and their real-people problems; he also fully embodied that message in his life in this real world. He thereby showed us that his "kingdom" was no dreamy fantasy but a place to be lived in here and now.

> ## He thereby showed us that his "kingdom" was no dreamy fantasy but a place to be lived in here and now.

In order to do something about the human problem, Jesus had to become human and had to be present in this world. As the Letter to the Hebrews puts it, if Jesus was God With Us, God doing something decisive about the problem between us and God, then "he had to be made like his brothers and sisters in every way" (2:17). Only a fully human Savior can save us in our full humanity and redeem all of us, who we are on Sunday in church and who we are on Monday at work.

At the same time, in order to do something about the human problem, Jesus was more than human. The Gospel writers strain to speak of his strange human-and-more-than-human quality. An embarrassing pregnancy, inexplicable signs and wonders—something's afoot among us that is bigger than us.

Rather than accommodate himself or his message to the limits of his audience, Jesus intensifies the oddness. "You have heard that it was said . . . but I say to you . . ." (Matt. 5:38) was a favorite phrase. A Messiah who avoids the powerful and the prestigious and goes to the poor and dispossessed? A way of life that begins in death, maturity that occurs only when one turns and becomes like "a little child" (Matt. 18:3), a Savior who is rejected by many whom he sought to save, a King who reigns from a bloody cross?

Christians believe that this story, for all its strangeness, is true. Here we have a truthful account of how our God wrote us back into the story of God. This is a truthful depiction not only of who God really is but also of how we who were lost got found, we enslaved got redeemed, we the dead restored, we the sorrowful damned rescued by a God who refused to let our rejection and rebellion (our notorious, long-term God problem) be the final word on matters between us and God. God With Us in order to be God For Us.

Jesus the Christ ("Christ" means "Messiah," "The Anointed One") was a human being born in a human family; attended parties (no one ever accused him of being too spiritual or too pious; critics sneered that he was a vulgar glutton and drunkard); moved constantly around the area of Galilee; ran afoul of governmental and religious authorities; taught through homely but disconcerting, pithy parables; did a number of surprising and utterly inexplicable "signs and wonders;" and eventually was tortured to death in a horribly cruel punishment that the Romans used against rebellious troublemakers.

A few days later, Jesus' astonished followers went public with the proclamation that Jesus had been raised from the dead and had returned to them, commissioning them to continue his work here and now.

While these are roughly the historical facts of Jesus from Nazareth, the raw facts don't tell the whole story. From the first, many knew that Jesus was not only a perceptive, challenging teacher ("rabbi," teacher, was a favorite designation for Jesus) but was also uniquely God present ("Emmanuel," means "God is with us"). In a very short time, Paul (whose letters are the earliest New Testament writings) acclaimed crucified and resurrected Jesus as the long-awaited Messiah, the Christ, the full revelation of God. Jesus was not only a loving and wise teacher; Jesus was God Almighty doing something decisive about the rift between us creatures and the Creator, infinity became finite, God With Us, the key to God's nature and intentions for the world. Jesus' people were unified in their conviction that they had seen "all the fullness of God was pleased to live in him" (Col. 1:19), a life completely at one with and fully transparent to God.

Jesus lived a life completely at one with and fully transparent to God.

God in Action

In Jesus the reign of God broke through to the world. He doesn't only make the reality of God's reign visible but also makes it possible. He not only healed people as sign of the future Kingdom's coming, but he also invited sinners and outcasts to join that kingdom now. He rendered God's coming kingdom not as some fuzzy future possibility, but as a raucous party in the present. To participate in that Kingdom was to be in the company of Jesus and to trust that what Jesus said about God and us was true, to live lives that showed that this God—rather than any of the then-popular godlets of the age like Dionysius, Artemis, Mars, Venus, Psyche, or Caesar—was in charge.

> He rendered God's coming kingdom not as some fuzzy future possibility, but as a raucous party in the present.

When they "believed in Jesus," they did not simply believe that he had some good ideas but that by his action and his invitation he had made a decisive difference in human history. God is doing what Jesus does.

In Jesus, God was not only revealing but acting. Thus Stephen, the first Christian martyr, without hesitation prays *to Jesus* (Acts 7:59) as he dies. Those fervent Jewish monotheists who had woken up each morning and prayed the beautiful Shema, "Hear, O Israel: The LORD our God is one . . ." (KJV) now routinely prayed to Jesus as the same, one God. They now gave answer to those who had asked, "Who is this that the winds and waves obey him?" or "Who is this who presumes to forgive sins?"

Who is this? None other than God, the one and only God of Israel, with us, God doing for us that which we could not do for ourselves.

If, simplistically, we say that Christ is "only human," then he has no more to tell us about God than the average, well-meaning, inspired spiritual teacher. However, if Christ is only God, then he has little relevance to this frail, finite, fragile thing called human life. Once God Almighty so unreservedly joined humanity in Jesus Christ, we were forced into complex conjunctive thinking—Jesus is *both* human *and* divine.

Try to evade the deity of Christ by making Jesus another victim of human injustice nailed to a cross and you leave God in heaven, a distant deity trapped in godliness. Belief in God becomes difficult; belief that God is concerned with your life becomes impossible. To fail at conjunctive thinking and lose the deity of Christ also means that we lose faith in humanity. It is one thing to believe that humanity is created in the image of God, but a much more blessed thing to believe that in spite of all our sin, God preserves that divine-human bond.

Christian theology is an ages-long attempt to keep the faith as complicated and conjunctive as it must be in order to do justice to the God who has met us in Jesus Christ. For instance, G. W. Hegel (1770–1831) was a philosopher who attempted to grapple with the intellectual challenges the modern world posed for the Christian faith. Christianity is true, said Hegel, but it is true in much the same way that a picture is true. Christian theology is a human representation or depiction of a truth, a reality that is other than that which the picture struggles to present.

Hegel said that the birth stories of Jesus are not accurate historical reports. They are pictures of the unfolding of God's life in our space and time (from primitive thesis, to challenging antithesis, to a better, higher synthesis). Judaism, said Hegel, was a first step in which God is depicted as an oriental potentate, distant and fearful (thesis). In the next phase God becomes a particular man, Jesus, who disrupts our notions of God (antithesis) so that we can progress to the final phase, "religion of the Spirit," in which God is spread to all and we come to understand the gradual unfolding of history as the working out of God's benevolent intentions for the world (synthesis). Don't get hung up on the Jewishness of Jesus, the miracles he performed, or other primitive (according to modern thinkers like Hegel) hindrances to belief; Christian theology is a pictorial way of speaking about deeper, constantly progressing spiritual realities.

Reacting against the paltry results of nineteenth-century historical research's attempts to recover the real "historical Jesus," Hegel postulated that what was really significant about Jesus was not the crude historical (human) facts of his life and work but rather Jesus as a forward advance in the unfolding of a grander, deeper (divine) Age of the Spirit.

Hegel's philosophy of religion later became known as "panentheism," or in its American version, "process theology." Pantheism has long taught that everything in the world is divine. Panentheism is a bit more sophisticated in teaching that everything is *in* God and that God can be found in all things. In pantheism God is no longer the Creator of the world, distinct from the world God has created, but rather God infuses all the world. God's engagement in history is less important than God as an idea above the grubby particularities of time and space.

Even as I attempt to describe the basics of Hegel's panentheism, you may be thinking that you have previously encountered Hegelianism and didn't know it. Much of what passes for "Creation Spirituality," or

"New Age Spirituality" these days is panentheism in new garb. If we are thinking about God, or matters of the spirit, there must be a way to think without recourse to the grubby particularities of earthly matters, so Hegelians of every age have argued. Religion progresses (or more accurately, recesses) into ever more vague platitudes, ever more distant from the death and decay of worldly existence.

Kierkegaard smirked that if Hegel was right about the Spirit's unfolding in history, ascending up a vague, philosophical set of misty ideas, isn't it odd that when God was born among us God chose to be born as a rudimentarily educated Jewish peasant and not as a modern German philosopher?

Against the Hegelians, Kierkegaard countered that Christianity is rooted and takes its stand in a bloody cross, a historical fact, not some high-flown philosophical idea. The crucifixion of Christ was not a primitive (Jewish) stage that we have at last risen above, not another miscarriage of justice by a despotic government; the cross is the God-ordained summit beyond which no one can ascend, the deepest truth to be told about the heart of Israel's God. There is no God hiding behind events of the life and death of Jesus. There, on the cross, is as much of God as we ever hope to see. Jesus is more than an insightful teacher who was the highest and best product of human aspiration, up through the first century. Christians know him as the decisive, conclusive presence of God With Us, God as God is, God self-disclosed, not our highest concept of God but rather God's lowest descent to us.

There is no veil we must lift and peek behind, no set of undiscovered sacred texts, no archaeological discovery yet to be made that can tell us more than God has graciously revealed to us about Christ. Of course, knowing about Christ—facts and figures, the stuff of human knowing—is not enough. Post-Resurrection, we "know" Christ as fully human and fully divine by a way of knowing that is more adventurous than most of what passes for knowledge in the modern world. Only faith can lead us to be able to declare with the whole church down through the ages, "God was reconciling the world to himself through Christ" (2 Cor. 5:19).

> # Faith is the name for what happens when human reason encounters and submits to the nature and reality of God as God is self-disclosed in Jesus Christ.

Faith is the name for what happens when human reason encounters and submits to the nature and reality of God as God is self-disclosed in Jesus Christ. Fortunately for sincere seekers after God, the Incarnation demonstrates that we have a God who relentlessly self-discloses.

God Is Greater Than Our Desires

When people like us say "God," we're usually applying "god" to a set of ideas devised by modern Western culture called "Moralistic, Therapeutic Deism." Our religion tends to be moralistic—everything reduced to ethics, the gospel transformed from something God has done for us into a moral program to be followed by us.

A primary attribute of this "god" is usefulness in our various projects. We live in a utilitarian, pragmatic age where all truth is judged by "What's in it for me?" No wonder that many disbelievers reject what we have made of "god," because our "god" sounds suspiciously like a personal assistant we have concocted for ourselves. Religion is now commended not because it is true but because it is good for us.

Our culturally acceptable god-who-is-no-God is not only moralistically, therapeutically designed but also deistic. Deism was all the rage during John Wesley's day. Wesley, one of the most irenic of theologians, expressed contempt for the desiccated, flaccid god-who-isn't-much-of-a-God of the Deists. What to do when the thought forms of the modern world could not easily comprehend the demanding, sovereign, intruding-at-the-most-inopportune-times Incarnate God of Scripture? Emphasize that aspect of God that is allegedly accessible to human reason—God Creator of the world. Founding fathers like Washington and Jefferson were Deists. When founding a new democratic nation where the people are sovereign, a God who creates the world and then retires is as much of a "god" as we can handle. Brilliant slaveholder Thomas Jefferson had to be nervous about an incarnating God who stands in judgment upon human behavior, and who by coming in the flesh redeemed all people as children of God.

An aloof, allegedly caring but inactive, spiritual, vague deity is perfectly designed for modern Western people who have been conditioned to organize the world around themselves. A self-fabricated "god" (that is, *idol*) is always easier to get along with than the true and living God who is considerably more than a figment of our imagination. The shear strangeness of the Doctrine of the Incarnation makes it difficult to say that here is an idea of God that we came up with on our own.

"Well, you're Catholic and I'm Baptist," I overheard one student say to another. "Whatever works for you." "You don't know much about Catholics," I was surprised to overhear the student respond. "Sometimes I can't stand being Catholic. It's not working for me; it's working *on* me. But it is not working for me."

Christians don't claim that a complex notion like Incarnation is helpful; we simply know it is true. Be warned: exploring the Incarnation, working through this book, risks having a most demanding God work on us.

I know a theologically and politically conservative pastor who has challenged the governor and legislature of Alabama on its draconian anti-immigration laws. He has become a fierce critic and passionate activist for voiceless, undocumented immigrants. Why?

"Our Lord Jesus Christ, whom we know to be the full revelation of God, was an immigrant to Egypt when he was a baby. Furthermore, he has commanded us to show hospitality to the sojourner and stranger. That's why I fight for the rights of immigrants."

Such are the perils of believing that in Jesus Christ, God was reconciling the world to himself.

Chapter 2

Now, a Word from God

Ahaz, King of Judah, has a problem. A large force is arrayed against him (Isaiah 7).

"Ask a sign from the LORD your God," advises the prophet Isaiah. "The Lord will give you a sign. The young woman is pregnant and is about to give birth to a son, and she will name him Immanuel." The child will be a sign of divine favor.

Ahaz surely thought to himself, *I need chariots, warriors, swords, and all you have to offer is a nameless pregnant woman and a baby?*

The King of Judah thought that he and his adversaries were the only actors on the stage of history. He was wrong. God is active here, now, yet active in a way that is peculiar to this God.

God shows up, our prayers are answered, but not always in the way we expected.

Early Christians maintained their Jewish faith that there is only one God. Jesus was not a new God who had superseded the old, but rather in Jesus, the God whom Israel had always struggled to worship, believe, and obey was now revealed in human form. When Christians read the Old Testament (the Bible of Jesus), it was therefore quite natural to see the activity and identity of the God of Israel as prefigurement of Jesus.

God made a covenant with Abraham. And yet the Hebrews languished in Egyptian slavery. Exodus reports God's intervention: "The Israelites were still groaning because of their hard work. They cried out, and their cry to be rescued from the hard work rose up to God. God heard their cry of grief, and God remembered his covenant with Abraham, Isaac, and Jacob. God looked at the Israelites, and God understood" (Exod. 2:23-25).

God not only notices but shows up, intervenes, and enlists the aid of Moses to bring the Israelites to freedom. Note that when Yahweh appears to Moses, Moses responds with a simple, "I'm here" (Exod. 3:4), a similar response as that of the Virgin Mary to the intruding angel (Luke 1:38). Mary's response was formed by a faith that had tutored her to expect God to show up in unexpected times and places, enlisting unexpected people to perform unexpected signs and wonders.

When Jesus appears, it is this God with whom Jesus is identified. While the embodiment of God in a historical person, at a particular time and place, is claimed uniquely for Jesus, I hope you see that his Incarnation is not out of God's character. This God shows up.

The Incarnation affirms God's particularity; God's propensity to show up at a particular time and place; God's choice of a distinct people, Israel; and God's calling and use of specific individuals to accomplish God's purposes for the whole world. As Paul told one of his congregations, "God chose what the world considers low-class and low-life" to do God's work in the world (1 Cor. 1:28).

We are forever saying that we want God to show up. "If only you would tear open the heavens and come down!" pleads the prophet (Isa. 64:1). We find ourselves in a mess and know that the mess is so great that no one could get us out but God. A consistent biblical claim is that God always shows up, not always when we demand, but shows up nevertheless.

Not the God We Expected

Trouble is, when God shows up—not as the God we presumed, but as the God who is—that's another matter. Many in the first century prayed for a Messiah, the Anointed Holy One of God, to come and fix things. Some, when they met Jesus, scoffed, "That's not how a Messiah is supposed to look. We were praying for a military leader who would march in, run the Romans out of Judea, and set up a new King David government. We got a carpenter's son from Nazareth.

In Luke 4, Jesus shows up one Sabbath at his hometown synagogue at Nazareth. They hand him the scroll of the prophet Isaiah. He reads the beloved words promising God's deliverance of Israel:

> *The Spirit of the Lord is upon me,*
> *because the Lord he has anointed me.*
> *He has sent me to preach good news*
> *to the poor,*
> *to proclaim release to the prisoners*
> *and recovery of sight to the blind,*
> *to liberate the oppressed.*

(Luke 4:18-19)

An excited stir in the congregation. After all, who is more oppressed and deserving of release than us, languishing here with the heel of Rome on our necks? It's about time that God incarnated among us. The young rabbi begins to preach, drawing upon the stories of God's appearances through the work of the prophets.

"There were many widows in Israel during Elijah's time. . . . Yet Elijah was sent to none of them. . . . There were also many persons with skin diseases in Israel during the time of the prophet Elisha, but none of them were cleansed. Instead, Naaman the Syrian was cleansed" (Luke 4:25-26).

Congregational adoration turned to murderous wrath. Who asked for a preacher to remind us that God had blessed the wrong people before and might well do so again?

These days, the challenge of believing the Doctrine of Incarnation is not in believing that God might come. After all, we are such adorable creatures, we modern people. The challenge today is the same as it has always been in our reception of God: to receive God *as God comes to us.* The jolt is not so much that God was in Christ, reconciling the world to himself; it's that God was in *Christ.*

> # The challenge today is . . . to receive God as *God comes to us.*

God Says the Word

In the beginning was the Word and the Word was with God and the Word was God. The Word was with God in the beginning. Everything came into being through the Word, and without the Word nothing came into being. What came into being through the Word was life, and the life was the light for all people. The light shines in the darkness, and the darkness doesn't extinguish the light. . . . The Word became flesh and made his home among us.

We have seen his glory, glory like that of a father's only son, full of grace and truth. . . . No one has ever seen God. God the only Son, who is at the Father's side, has made God known. (John 1:1-5, 14, 18)

John's Gospel begins by designating Christ as "the Word." All God has to do to bring forth something out of nothing is to say the word (Genesis 1). John says that the creating "Word" was even before creation and now that primal, world-making Word has come to us. Immediate implications of this majestic prologue:

(1) our words are not the first word

(2) we have been addressed

(3) we are not alone

The identity of Word became flesh awaits full revelation in the remainder of John's Gospel. The truth that "no one has ever seen God" is countered with the promise that "God the only Son . . . has made God known" (1:18). The Fourth Gospel has no birth narrative: no manger and no virgin birth. The nativity stories in Matthew and Luke report on the event of Incarnation; John's theological, poetic prologue says what the event means.

The meaning of things, said Greek philosophy, the logic behind it all, is the *logos* (Greek *logos,* "word"). The opening words of John's Gospel claim in a very Jewish way that "in the beginning was the Word." The Eternal Logos, the reason for everything, the heart of the matter, the source of all things, is the Word—Christ. John uses worldly philosophy to make heavenly affirmation. And yet in doing so, John speaks about something beyond the reach of worldly philosophy, namely, the very Jewish notion that God, in love, shows up.

God, in Love, Shows Up

"The Word (*logos*) became flesh" is a stunning declaration of God's availability. A word becomes flesh and blood? The incomprehensible, wondrous logic of God has become a person? Yes, said Jesus' first followers. The One who created the world, the One whom Israel was reluctant even to set eyes upon, has become a human being. What matters most about God has become matter. Meaning has become material. As Luke might put it, the logic of the universe is embodied in a tiny baby. Or, as John says (literally, in the Greek, John 1:14), "The Word has tented among us." The world was created for this stunning moment so that God could tabernacle among us in Jesus Christ.

The Christian faith is not common sense, not even a noble philosophy of life. It's about the reality of that person, God fully God, embodied, up close and personal as a Jew from Nazareth.

As someone who has taught at a university, I learned firsthand the oddness of Jesus majestically pronouncing, "I am the way, the truth, and the life" (John 14:6). In academia truth is more typically regarded as a notion, an abstract idea, a universal generality.

But Jesus says, "*I am the truth.*" The truth is personal, a person. We didn't choose this truth; he chose us. That is a very odd definition of truth.

In one of his aphorisms, Nietzsche asks, "What if truth was a woman?" The question sounds sexist, and Nietzsche was not above sexism. And yet it raises the possibility that truth might not be dry, detached, desiccated ideas but rather intuitive, emotional, embodied, demanding, and personal. In short, what if truth is a Jew from Nazareth who lived briefly, died violently, and rose unexpectedly?

Into the primal darkness, God says "light" and a benighted chaos comes alive (Genesis 1). John's Gospel begins with that word "genesis"—"In the beginning . . ." Jesus is light like the first light of creation. Later in this Gospel, Jesus will call himself "light of the world" (8:12; 12:35). The advent of Jesus Christ is Genesis 1–2, creation of a new world, all over again.

And yet John's Gospel does more than simply announce the advent of Light. John also admits (1:5) that the "light shines in the darkness, and the darkness doesn't extinguish the light." Jesus intrudes into the world's chaos and evil. The NRSV says that the darkness "did not overcome" the light, a good rendering of the

Greek *katalambano*. I also like the old KJV rendering of *katalambano* as "the darkness comprehended it not."

John delights in the use of double entendre, therefore we are justified in rendering *katalambano* as either "overcome" or as "comprehend." The darkness has been unable either fully to comprehend or finally to overcome the brightness of the Light of the World.

Perhaps last Sunday there was a respectable number at your church to worship God. But even a big crowd is still a minority of people in town. Most of these non-attenders are not hostile to the Christian faith; they just don't get it. For them, Christmas is a holiday, a grand time to eat and to drink too much, to spend too much, and to travel too far. When Christians gather to sing, "Joy to the world, the Lord has come!" the majority of the world he came to save just doesn't get it. The people "comprehend it not."

God, having tried to speak to us down through the ages, in the Incarnation at last "spoke to us through a Son" (Heb. 1:2). But most people look at Jesus and see only a historical figure who said a few interesting things and then faded into obscurity. They "comprehend it not." The world that the Word created did not know him. He lived among his own, and his own didn't receive him. What a sad irony: God finally speaks clearly, decisively, an embodied word, and the world comprehends it not.

Although John will not again refer to Jesus as the Word, John surely means for these majestic cadences to stick in our minds as we read the rest of the Christ story. For instance, John introduces Jesus at, of all places, a wedding; more accurately, the bash after the wedding (John 2:1-11). During the festivities, the wine runs out. Jesus' mother anxiously tells him that the wine is gone. Jesus brusquely replies, "What does that have to do with me?" "Do whatever he tells you," Mary says to the servants. Jesus tells them to fill the stone water jars to the brim. The water is turned to wine.

John says this was "the first miraculous sign" and that "his disciples believed in him." The first of his "signs," his first wonder, produced 180 gallons of wine? What's the spiritual good in that? And what on earth did his disciples believe about him? It is only the second chapter of the Fourth Gospel; Jesus has not yet preached or taught. And yet, whereas most of the people at the party observing the miracle probably scratched their heads saying, "How did he do that?" a few came away from this weird moment believing in Jesus.

Little is explained. Questions remain. Whenever the Incarnate Word is present, even at an allegedly secular occasion such as a post-wedding bash, expect the unexpected. And expect confusion. In all this, John surely wants to say, "Welcome to the world now that the Word has become flesh."

It's a marvel that anybody encountered the Word Made Flesh and said, "This is God's eternal word spoken to us." It's a theme—listening but not hearing, looking but not seeing—that recurs in the Fourth Gospel. Jesus, the Living Word, speaks, but people just don't get it. "Wow! That's a hard word," say his own disciples when he tells them that he is the bread come down from heaven whom they must devour (John 6). "What does he mean?" asks the baffled mob in Jerusalem (7:36), and Jesus sardonically says, "There is no place in you for my word. . . . It is because you cannot accept my word" (8:37, 43 NRSV).

So if my exposition of the Incarnation is incomprehensible, relax; take heart. That's a typical reaction to the Word Made Flesh. If, however, as strange as this word sounds, you hear an address to you, John says that you are a new creation; like Genesis 1–2 all over again, the light really does shine in the darkness for you. "Those who did welcome him, those who believed in his name, he authorized to become God's children, born not from blood nor from human desire or passion, but born from God" (John 1:12). Furthermore, if you stick with these words, words that you cannot speak to yourself, they become the very source of your life: "If you continue in my word . . . you will know the truth, and the truth will make you free" (John 8:31 NRSV). These words proclaim God's gracious solution to the problem between you and God: "You have already been cleansed by the word that I have spoken to you" (John 15:3 NRSV). You are a new creation. You carry God's light with you in a dark world.

> ## You are a new creation. You carry God's light with you in a dark world.

The Greek *katalambano* can be rendered in yet one more way than "comprehend" or "overcome." It could also be, "The darkness has not overtaken it." The darkness doesn't "get it" in the sense that the darkness doesn't grasp the Light. In John 12, Jesus warns his disciples to walk in the light lest the darkness "overtake you." Same verb—*katalambano*.

I asked a director of our town's ministry to the homeless what her greatest challenge is. She answered, "We are always one step ahead of financial disaster." And yet that same person who is constantly under threat of being overtaken by the darkness celebrated her tenth year as director of this ministry. The darkness has not overtaken the light.

I've seen the world try to turn a child into a grasping, materialistic, self-centered dolt, the embodiment of some people's "American Dream," only to watch God work through the church to transform that child into a caring, compassionate Christian. The world tried to overtake the Light of the World, and surprise, the world got overtaken!

Paul says in Romans 12 that we should not "be defeated by evil, but defeat evil with good." In other words, we respond to evil in the world as God has responded in Christ. Let light shine. We don't overcome evil with the ways of the world—through force, violence, retribution, or lying. We overcome evil as did Christ—love showing up, light shining into our benighted cosmos.

> # We respond to evil in the world as God has responded in Christ.

Hopeful and Realistic

Incarnation enables us to be both hopeful and realistic. We have seen the Light that means to shine everywhere; for us a new world has dawned but not completely, not yet. Incarnation is not only about the birth of a baby at Bethlehem but also about the brutal crucifixion of an innocent man on Golgotha. We didn't know how far God intended to take Incarnation until we stood at the foot of the cross. "Love came down at Christmas," as we sometimes sing, and love also came down on Good Friday.

Many have accused mainline, liberal Protestantism of a too-sanguine view of evil. When it comes to our views of human nature, we tend to think of ourselves as basically nice people who are making progress through our education, our enlightened attitudes, and our social programs for good. Advocates of the "Prosperity Gospel" urge people to use their faith to plug into the "good life," as the world defines the good life, without any gospel critique of the world.

We can only regard the present world as unadulteratedly "good" by denying the evil that runs rampant, the suffering of the innocent, and the unrelieved injustice that afflicts so many. The Light will overcome all the forces set against it, but the meantime may not be pretty. There will be suffering and blood before the full story of the babe of Bethlehem ends, Good Friday follows Christmas, and Jesus promises his followers not a cushion but a cross.

Therefore, as the church sings its joy, it must take care to admit to the sadness still among us. When the church exclusively puts on a happy face and cheerily celebrates the light, the joy, and the victory without also being honest about the struggle and the defeat, we do the Incarnation an injustice and we alienate our proclamation of Christ from some of the hurting people Christ means to love.

The Light of the World does not avoid or deny the reality of the darkness; in the Incarnation, the Light enters into and works within the realm of sin, and ultimately triumphs. That is one reason we call the words of the Eternal Word "gospel." The Light of the World shines in the darkness, and the darkness has not overcome it, comprehended it, or overtaken it!

> # The Light of the World shines in the darkness and the darkness has not overcome it, comprehended it, or overtaken it!

As the Word spoken by the prophets, made manifest in the commandments, become flesh in Jesus Christ, the Word is then preached and given flesh and blood in the preaching, hearing, and active witness of the congregation. When you consider all of the possibilities against the faith, it's amazing that so many—when faced with a strange, inexplicable wonder like Incarnation—comprehend the truth, believe, and bow before it. That you are taking the trouble to read this book about the Incarnation, that you are able to stand and sing at the Feast of the Nativity, "Hark! the herald angels sing, 'Glory to the newborn King,'" is a virtual proof of the reality of Incarnation.

Shine, Jesus shine.

Chapter 3

Help Is on the Way

Steve Seamands reports that the *St. Petersburg Times* published a paper on Christmas Day that said, "In keeping with the Christmas spirit, only good news will appear on the front page. For a full report on other happenings around the world, see page 3A." Sure enough, on the front page there was a picture of the pope, a story of a family helping another family in need, and Santa Claus stretched out on a patio, soaking in Florida sun. Then the rest of the news: freedom fighters in Cuba in retreat, a stickup in Chicago, the perishing of a family of nine in a fire, civil war in the Congo, and assorted tragedies from around the globe. Seamands counters that the well-intentioned newspaper editor missed the point of Christmas: "Jesus, the Son of God, wasn't born into a sentimental, good-news-*only* fantasy world. He was born into *this* world, *our* world, which was evil and dangerous then just as it is now."[1]

It is scandal enough that God should become human, should be born of a woman in an out-of-the-way place. But that incarnational scandal is deepened, intensified, in that God experiences death in the most shameful form as an executed criminal. Thus Christians answered the question, "Who is God?" by pointing to the cross and stating what they had learned about God through Jesus: "God is love" (1 John 4:8).

"Whoever has seen me has seen the Father" (John 14:9) is an astounding thing for someone to say about himself, especially if that person speaks and acts like Jesus. In claiming that when we see him we see God, Jesus becomes the test of all of our statements about God. We thought God was at last stirring to save us from our enemies, entering the capital city to defeat our Roman overlords. Jesus enters the city bouncing on the back of a donkey, welcomed not by the powers that be but rather by little children shouting, "Hosanna!" In so doing, Jesus rearranges our ideas about God.

> In claiming that when we see him we see God, Jesus becomes the test of all of our statements about God.

Thinking Faithfully about Christ

Quite early on, the church realized that to get Christ wrong is to get God wrong. It took us four centuries to find ideas commensurate with the reality of Incarnation. We tried simpler solutions but none of them worked.

Adoptionism: Jesus was a wonderfully God-intoxicated human being, anointed by the Holy Spirit in much the same way as the prophets of the Old Testament, only more so. At his baptism, Adoptionists asserted, Jesus was "adopted" by the Father and became God the Father's beloved Son, commissioned to preach the good news and to perform miracles in the name of the Father. Jesus is almost like God, but not quite.

Docetism (from the Greek, *dokein,* "to appear"), in contrast to Adoptionism, said that Christ was fully divine but from time to time "appeared" to be human. Docetism fails to acknowledge Christ's full humanity— it is inconceivable that an omniscient and omnipotent God could suffer human pain on the cross. Christ lovingly appeared to humanity as if he were one of us, but spiritually insightful believers know that he was actually God in human disguise. Jesus was much like a human being, but not quite.

Sometimes the church has focused upon Jesus' birth, death, and resurrection and has neglected an emphasis upon his life and ministry. This is a docetic limitation of the truth of Incarnation. When we think about a real human being, we don't just focus upon a vague image of what he or she looks like; we also focus upon what he or she says and does. That Jesus was born of the Virgin Mary tells us something important about him; how he acted as an adult tells us even more. Jesus didn't just enunciate a few high-sounding principles; he became a model for us to follow, a teacher who led by example. "I am the way, the truth, and the life," says Jesus in John's Gospel (14:6). In saying, "I am the way," Jesus is surely speaking about the totality of his life and work here on this earth. We are to walk the way he walked. Neglect of Jesus' life and work by exclusively focusing upon his birth, cross, and resurrection is Docetism in yet another guise.

Some popular contemporary preachers present sermons that extract kernel principles and noble ideas of contemporary relevance from the primitive husk of biblical narratives, as if the historical particularities of Jesus' life and death don't matter, as if how Jesus actually lived in this world is detached from the alleged principles he taught. Or take, for example, the infamous Jesus Seminar, makes a big deal of voting up or down what the members judge to be the actual words of Jesus, as if we worship the words of Jesus. Docetism lives!

We say in the Nicene Creed that Jesus "suffered under Pontius Pilate." That is, Jesus engaged in the most universal and unavoidable of human conditions: pain. Any docetic attempt to back off from Jesus' suffering, attempting to redo Jesus into some sort of impervious robot who was born and then died, and whose bodily and spiritual suffering are only illusions, has always been resisted by the church.

Jesus gave his followers absolutely no permission ever to impose suffering upon others, yet at the same time promised that they would encounter suffering because of him. In 1 Peter 2:21 we are told: "You were called to this kind of endurance, because Christ suffered on your behalf. He left you an example so that you might follow in his footsteps." A docetic, almost human Christ tends to be irrelevant to human suffering. The Scriptures say that Christ did not just come close to human suffering and mortality but also dared to drink the cup of suffering all the way to the dregs. Down through the ages, countless Christians have discovered the pastoral truth of the Incarnation: only a truly human, suffering Savior can help.

Against Docetists of every age, G. K. Chesterton wrote, "Orthodox theology has specifically insisted that Christ was not a being apart from God and man, like an elf, nor yet a being half human and half not, like a centaur, but both things at once and both things thoroughly, very man and very God."[2]

Arianism (from a fourth-century cleric, Arius) was the main cause for convening the great fourth-century ecumenical councils that affirmed the Incarnation. Arianism, professing great admiration for God the Father, said that God's essence could not be shared, for such sharing would entail a division and diminution of God. Arius reasoned that Christ, the Eternal Word of God, can't be fully one with God, but must be a creature formed by the Father. "Son of God" is therefore a sort of honorary title because of Christ's superior character. Like the Adoptionists, Arius stressed Christ's humanity, saying that though he was a human being, Christ was the highest and best of all God's creatures, nearly God, but not quite.

While orthodox Christianity rejected Arianism, like Docetism it never disappeared. Pick something about Jesus that you find appealing and emphasize that virtue as making Jesus very special. Those well-meaning folk who acclaim Jesus as a man of high moral character or a great ethical teacher or a spiritual leader or an example of God's love and justice in service to the poor (though not really "God") show the resilience of Arianism. Arians tend to see Jesus as a teacher or "Spirit person" (e.g., theologian and author Marcus Borg); Jesus' teaching is more important than Jesus himself. Jesus becomes a great example, among other human examples, of compassion and spiritual wisdom. The cross is reduced to an evil act done to Jesus rather than a human act that a redemptive God used to do something about us. The mysterious story of our redemption, the cross, is reduced to a sad tale of yet another good teacher whose teaching brought him to a bad conclusion.

Against all these attempts to make God With Us more accessible to our conventional thinking, in 451 CE the Council of Chalcedon worked out an elegantly philosophical defense of Jesus Christ as fully human and fully divine. The Nicene Creed, and the more fully developed Constantinopolitan Creed that came shortly after it, refused to attempt to encase Christ in any sensible, logical, but (in regard to what we know of Christ) simplistic and heretical attempt to conceive of the meaning of Christ. Much was at stake. Nothing within us can save us; we can be rescued, redeemed, and enlightened only by God. In Christ, Chalcedon reasoned, God was rescuing and redeeming humanity, not simply working through a representative or highly placed emissary of God. At the same time our Redeemer must become fully like us in order fully to redeem all of us.

Chalcedon did not attempt precisely to define how Christ is fully human and fully divine, rather the council affirmed what the church had always known about Jesus Christ. Christ presents us with many tensions— the tension between our ways and God's way, friction between the kingdom of God and the kingdoms of this earth, contrasts between present life and eternal life. Chalcedon blessed the tension that had been part of our encounter with Jesus from the first, letting the tension stand forever as a rebuke to any simplistic way of speaking about Christ.

Chesterton said that in our thought about the Incarnation, "Christianity got over the difficulty of combining furious opposites by keeping them both, and keeping them both furious."[3] I'm glad that, in thinking about Christ, the church in its wisdom did not falsely harmonize or overly simplify if this conjunctive truth but allowed to stand the "furious opposites" combined so wondrously in Christ.

The Doctrine of the Incarnation is opposed to all theories that surmise Jesus as a mere theophany, a transitory appearance by God in human form, such as we often meet among the world's religions. In contrast, Incarnation asserts that there is an inextricable, abiding union between Jesus as Son of God and Jesus as fully Son of Man. So-called progressive Christianity, successor to liberal Christianity, seems prone to view Jesus as a fine revelation for his time, but one that can be surpassed in humanity's ever progressing sense of God. No, says orthodox Christianity. Jesus is actually the full truth about God, God's descent to us because we could not progress up toward God.

Because God so fully loved the world, we may love as well. Christian faith is never exclusively, or even primarily, about some future positive condition. Because of the Incarnation, we've got to love the world now, in the spirit of Christ love the world we've got, because the Incarnation proves that God has got the world. Eternal life (at least in John's Gospel) is not some misty future destination. Eternal life is life lived now in light of the Word made flesh among us here and now. It's what life is like once Jesus, the Incarnate Word, shows up.

The Incarnation leads us to try to love the world, the whole world, half as much as God loves in Jesus Christ, following the same suffering, self-sacrificial way that Jesus loved. Jesus went to the cross praying, "Thy kingdom come. Thy will be done in earth, as it is in heaven" (Matt. 6:10 KJV), and taught us to do the same, loving the world as God presently loves the world, loving in the expectation of the final triumph of God's intentions for the world.

For Us and Our Salvation

"Who for us . . . and . . . our salvation . . . became human" is not just the heart of the Nicene-Constantinopolitan Creed; it is also at the heart of our faith's claims about Jesus. This is the discovery that led some pious Jews to break with tradition and preach to the world their belief that there are now two names for the powers that rule in heaven: the Father and the Son, who both reign in the power of the Holy Spirit. Why did Almighty God take on our humble flesh? "For us . . . and . . . our salvation."

John's first letter says, "Whoever does not love does not know God, for God is love. God's love was revealed among us in the way: God sent his only Son into the world so that we might live through him. In this is love, not that we loved God but that he loved us and sent his Son to be the atoning sacrifice for our sins" (1 John 4:8-10 NRSV).

Contemporary critics have charged Christians with a sort of anthropocentric narcissism. "How arrogant," they say, "that we humans should think that the Creator of the universe would go to so much trouble for the likes of us."

This is indeed the great scandal of the Incarnation—that a God of great magnitude, creator of "all things visible and invisible" (Nicene Creed), for the sake of us humans entered into our space and time in Christ and fully embraces humanity despite the cost.

Besides, to say that the Incarnation was "for us . . . and . . . our salvation" doesn't mean that God's love and salvific work is limited to us humans. Paul says the whole creation is groaning as it awaits deliverance (Rom. 8:19), suggesting that the saving work of God in Incarnation is more than individual; it's cosmic. Look at "God so loved the world that he gave his only Son, so that everyone who believes in him won't perish but will have eternal life" (John 3:16). Sometimes the church acts as if what Jesus said was, "For God so loved me and my church friends who resemble me . . ." thus limiting the scope of salvation in Incarnation.

The saving work of God in Incarnation is more than individual; it's cosmic.

The claim that, in Christ, "God so loved the world" led early Christians to bound beyond the geographic confines of Judea, charging throughout the world boldly making cosmic claims that seem all out of proportion to their small, beleaguered, disliked status in the empire. In just a few years after the Resurrection, these once disheartened disciples became apostles, witnesses "to the ends of the earth" (Acts 1:8) who busily made disciples of all nations (Matt. 28:19). His own experience of the Incarnation led Paul to tell the struggling little band at Corinth that even in their difficulties they must not forget that "the world, life, death, things in the present, things in the future—everything belongs to you, but you belong to Christ, and Christ belongs to God" (1 Cor. 3:22). It's a rather preposterous claim to make for the poor Corinthians—unless the Incarnation is true.

Marcus Borg says that if you think Jesus thought of himself as "one anointed by God to be the climactic figure in Israel's history," then "thinking that Jesus thought of himself in such grand terms raises serious questions about the mental health of Jesus." Borg declares, "I don't think people like Jesus have an exalted perception of themselves."[4]

Borg says we have two ways to think about Incarnation. The first way is "supernatural theism," which he dismisses as "common in popular-level Christianity throughout the centuries." He claims that this view naively "sees God as a being 'out there' and not 'here.'" God is seen as an "interventionist" who, for about three years, inserted Jesus "as the unique incarnation of an absent interventionist God."

The other view, which is Borg's, is "panentheism or dialectial theism." "God is not 'out there' but 'right here' as well as *more* than right here. Within this view, Jesus as a Spirit person was open to the presence of God. . . . I see Jesus as the embodiment and incarnation of the God who is everywhere present. But he is not a visitor from elsewhere, sent to the world by a god 'out there.' He is not different in kind from us but as completely human as we are."[5] Is Borg an Arian or Docetist? You make the call.

Borg generalizes the idea of Incarnation into a vague divine permeation of earthly things, detaching the presence of God from the specifics of Jesus. As we noted earlier, rendering Incarnation into a vague sense of God's presence in the world has long been a way to escape the potentially life-changing, challenging demands of Jesus by rendering him spiritual and insubstantial. The world was created by God, so the reasoning goes, and God loves us and the world enough to send the Son, therefore let us be content with ourselves as we are and the world as it is.

No. Incarnation is an aspect of the Atonement, God's setting right things between us and God. Bethlehem and Golgotha are linked. In Jesus Christ, God said a divine, dramatic, loving yes to us; the God of the cross also said a resounding, decisive no to how we were living and to what we made of the world. Christ loved us enough to become one with us as we are but Christ loved us enough not to leave us as we are. As the creed proclaims, he became incarnate "for us and our salvation," not simply to affirm our humanity or to condone our continued sin.

> In Jesus Christ, God said a divine, dramatic, loving yes to us. . . . The God of the cross also said a resounding, decisive no to how we were living.

Borg's pantheism is similar to Joan Osborne's popular song that goes, "What if God was one of us? . . . Just a stranger on the bus?" Incarnation stresses that God has indeed become like one of us, a full human being, but he also came to us *as Jesus,* a very specific human being who lived, died, and rose in a specific way. Furthermore, Jesus is more than "one of us;" he is at the same time the full, unique revelation of God, which none of us is or ever will be.

N. T. Wright admits that incarnational thinking "entails a commitment of faith, love, trust, and obedience" in the witness of Scripture. Borg has more confidence in his own insights about Jesus than do the testimonies of Matthew, Mark, or Luke. His Christology is his reflection upon his own spiritual experience rather than upon the specifics of Christ, because he sees the Gospels as products of human spirituality. Wright countered Borg by boldly stating, "I do not think . . . I am merely talking about the state of my own devotion. . . . I am talking . . . about Jesus and God."[6]

While we cannot ascend to God through our human thoughts and experiences, it is true that God descends to us, and when that happens, we indeed experience the truth of Incarnation. We bump against a God who is not merely a projection of our spiritual yearnings. Though the experience of millions confirms the Gospels' testimony of God With Us, the Gospels are more than testimony to inner human experience. In the rhythm of the church's worship, we experience Incarnation. The pattern of prayer and praise that we follow on Sunday morning is a very human activity that takes place in earthly space and time. We wash with water in baptism; we ingest wine and bread in the Eucharist. In so doing we become vulnerable to the incursions of a God we did not concoct for ourselves. We dare to believe that God uses these thoroughly human activities—bathing, eating, and drinking—to come very close to us in all of God's holy otherness.

> God uses these thoroughly human activities . . . to come very close to us.

We experience, maybe not every Sunday, but often enough to keep us at worship, the presence of God moving among us in our earthly worship. There we are, just going through the rituals, only to be surprised by the undeniable descent of the Holy Spirit. We find ourselves, as Charles Wesley wrote, "lost in wonder, love, and praise," and we exclaim with our progenitor, Jacob, an incarnational thought: "The LORD is definitely in this place, but I didn't know it" (Gen. 28:16).

Standing at the baptismal font, offering a dear child to be baptized, we look up and there at the font are all the desperate, degenerate, despicable rogues and knuckle-heads whom our Lord has gone out and recruited for the kingdom of God. We are making Eucharist, meeting Jesus in bread and wine, only to see across from us at the Lord's Table Judas—and worse. One reason we believe in the truth of Incarnation is not only because the Bible tells us so but also because we've lived it in your church and mine.

> We announce to you what existed from the beginning, what we have heard, what we have seen with our eyes, what we have seen and our hands handled, about the word of life. The life was revealed, and we have seen, and we testify and announce to you the eternal life that was with the Father and was revealed to us. What we have seen and heard, we also announce it to you so that you can have fellowship with us. Our fellowship is with the Father and with his Son, Jesus Christ. (1 John 1:1-3)

Martin Luther in the Larger Catechism, 1529, said although those who follow faiths other than Christianity might worship the one, true God, they had no way of knowing God's attitude toward them: "They cannot expect any love or blessing from Him. . . . For they have not the Lord Christ, and besides, are not illumined and favored by any gifts of the Holy Ghost." In other words, they do not know God Incarnate. The Incarnation not only tells us who God is but also God's intentions for us.

I asked a distinguished new church planter what virtue he most admired in a potential new church planter. "A robust theology of the Incarnation," he replied. "Only someone who believes that God is relentlessly reaching out to save the world has the drive to birth a new church."

God With Us is experienced as God For Us. It's a huge, complex thought to think that God became fully human and yet remained fully divine. Philip Yancey recalls J. B. Phillips's delightful story about the Incarnation:

> A senior angel is showing a very young angel around the splendors of the universe. They view whirling galaxies and blazing suns, and then flit across the infinite distances of space until at last they enter one particular galaxy of 500 billion stars: As the two of them draw near the star which we call our sun and to its circling planets, the senior angel pointed to a small and rather insignificant sphere turning very slowly on its axis. It looked as dull as a dirty tennis-ball to the little angel, whose mind was filled with the size and glory of what he had seen.
>
> "I want you to watch that one particularly," said the senior angel, pointing with his finger.
>
> "Well, it looks very small and rather dirty to me," said the little angel. "What's special about that one?"

He listened in stunned belief as the senior angel told him that this planet, small and insignificant
and not overly clean, was the renowned Visited Planet:

"Do you mean that our great and glorious Prince
. . . went down in Person to this fifth-rate little ball?
Why should He do a thing like that?"

The little angel's face wrinkled in disgust. "Do
you mean to tell me," he said, "that He stooped so
low as to become one of these creeping, crawling
creatures of that floating ball?"

"I do, and I don't think He would like you to
call them 'creeping, crawling creatures' in that tone
of voice. For, strange as it may seem to us, He loves
them. He went down to visit them to lift them up to
become like Him."

The little angel looked blank. Such a thought
was beyond his comprehension.[7]

That which is beyond our comprehension has made
itself available to us in a form that is not beyond our
experience. God is with us not only to reveal God to us
but also to be God for us.

I asked a pastor who visits the state prison every single week to conduct Bible study for the inmates why he
felt called to prison ministry. "I've not been given a great
deal of faith," he admitted. "Belief in Christ does not
come naturally to me. So I have to go where Jesus is. I

have to be sure that I stay close to Jesus. I feel so much closer to our Lord and find his presence so much more believable in prison than at church."

What a curious statement of faith—unless the Incarnation is true.

Life in the Light of Incarnation

Who can stand before this awesome truth of God With Us and not be changed in the meeting? Who can have this Light of the World shine upon them and not respond to the Light? The Incarnation is not proved in complex thinking but rather in faithful living as we attempt to embody in our earthly, human lives the divine mystery of the God who refused to be God without us.

> ## The Incarnation is not proved in complex thinking but rather in faithful living.

Julie Gold wrote a popular song, "From a Distance." You know how it goes: "God is watching us, God is watching us from a distance." Though a touching sentiment, it's against the whole point of Christianity. We were watching God "from a distance," thinking ourselves safe from the divine reach, hunkered down behind our self-constructed walls, clutching our stuff, secreted behind our brightly polished self-images. Then God came to us in Christ and risked loving us up close and personal. And for this. we nailed him to a cross.

Christian faith is the bold belief in God's thoroughgoing, costly engagement with the stuff of everyday life. This is good news for our contemporary "Age of Spirituality," as some have named it. In a time when many say, "I'm not religious, but I am very spiritual" (meaning, I've cranked down my religion to a vague, inner, ethereal feeling I keep mostly to myself), the time is never better to think Incarnation.

To one of his sorriest congregations Paul exclaimed, "Don't you know that you are God's temple and God's Spirit lives in you?" (1 Cor. 3:16). It's just what you would expect from a person who had been met by an incarnational God. Christ, the Light of the World, commissions us otherwise benighted ones to be lights to the world (Matt. 5:14). In so doing, Christ implies that if others are to experience the light of Christ, it will be through us. If we are to see God, we must see God through Christ; if the world is to know Christ, the world must learn of Christ through witnesses like us. Daunting thought.

My wife, Patsy, was leading a *DISCIPLE* Bible study. One week they read all the way through Leviticus.

When the group met to process what they had read, one of the members asked, "Why is God concerned about how we prepare meat, what we do with livestock, and women during their menstrual cycles? Does God have nothing better to do?" Another member of the group said, "I loved Leviticus because of its excruciating earthiness. I'm glad that God cares about what goes on in the kitchen, bedroom, and bath because that's where most of us spend most of our time. God doesn't just want my soul, and I don't have to be in church to serve God. Even at the kitchen sink, God is with us." A God who shows up, even in the kitchen amid pots and pans and dishwater, is inescapable.

Odd that we Christians sometimes present Christmas, the Feast of Incarnation, as something strange and mystical. Or else we self-righteously criticize everybody else for making the Yuletide so "materialistic." Christmas should be an annual reminder to a sometimes overly spiritualized church that Christianity *is* materialistic. God not only created matter; in Incarnation, God became material.

After having been met by the living God in the flesh of a Jew from Nazareth, we look for God at church *and* at the soup kitchen. Like the shepherds we seek God in angelic voices in the night sky *and* at a smelly cow stable. I expect to see something of Jesus in the dear saint at church *and* in the disagreeable, right-wing politician with whom I debate immigration policy.

A student friend spent a summer working as a volunteer in a Jesuit center for the homeless. Seven days a week, all day long, they offered free food, medical care, and counseling. At the end of a grueling day of beneficent activity, he and an old Jesuit priest finally closed the door to the center. As they did so, they peered out the window and saw yet one more shabby bag lady trudging down the walk toward the center. "Not another one!" exclaimed the tired student. "Jesus Christ!" "Could be, could be," muttered the priest as he sighed, unlocked the door, and welcomed yet another fellow human being in need who, because of Jesus, is also an instance of Incarnation.

Without Incarnation—God without a face or a name, God refusing to locate in a specific place and time—all you have is a tame, out-of-this-world, self-constructed Jesus (N. T. Wright calls it a *Da Vinci Code* Jesus) who doesn't challenge you here, now.

Before we end this incarnational excursion, let's tag some of the ways that the Doctrine of the Incarnation challenges us and makes a difference in the way we live.

Now That God Has Shown Up in Christ, We Expect to Meet God Everywhere

"Can anything from Nazareth be good?" they sneered when Jesus was presented to them (John 1:46). After God became incarnate in a dusty, undistinguished place like Bethlehem, expect God's incursions even where you live. We learned in Jesus that God is so completely loving, so determined to tabernacle and to have relationship with us that God shows up often at the most inopportune moments and in the most unlikely places. The Trinity is relentlessly determined to self-reveal.

> # The Trinity is relentlessly determined to self-reveal.

Have trouble believing Christian doctrine? Don't fret. Where just two or three of us gather, he promises to be there (Matt. 18:20). Having shown up to Mary, to Paul, to Matthew, Mark, and Luke, Jesus is sure to show up to you. The ability to believe and to respond in faithful discipleship is a gift an incarnate God lavishes upon us, "for us and for our salvation."

I know, I know. You have been conditioned to think that religion is something you do, a ritual or a good work you perform, some noble thought you have or noble sentiment you feel. The Incarnation, a gift given to us totally by God's initiative, reassures you that your relationship to God is God's self-assigned task. In Jesus Christ, God has decided to be for you, and God is faithful to God's promises. "They will be my people, and I will be their God," was the divine promise given

71

during one of Israel's most desperate hours (Jer. 24:7). That incarnational promise is shown to be kept not only throughout Scripture but also in your church and mine next Sunday. Even though we may wander from God, God in Jesus Christ refuses to be done with us.

> # The Incarnation, a gift given to us totally by God's initiative, reassures you that your relationship to God is God's self-assigned task.

The Incarnation challenges the current "Gospel of Success" of the televangelists, who say that signing on with Jesus leads to health, wealth, and no worries. They present Jesus as an effective means of achieving whatever it is that you want more than Jesus. Scripture teaches that Jesus is not a tool to get what we want but God's appointed means of getting what God wants. He comes to us not simply with blessings and benefits but also with assignments. His word was not, "Use me as a proven means of success in the world," but rather, "Follow me, and I'll give you outrageous assignments to do for God."

The great missionary bishop Lesslie Newbigin gave a Bible to an erudite Hindu friend. A few weeks later the friend returned the Bible complaining, "This is not a religious book. It hardly mentions the gods; it's filled with stories of ordinary and even bad people!"

If God incarnate should show up to enlist folk like Mary, Joseph, Peter, and Paul, well, what about you?

We Need Not Be More Spiritual Than Jesus

After Almighty God took on our flesh in Jesus Christ—assumed our body—bodies became forever blessed. Christians founded the first hospitals and pioneered in modern medicine; in the Incarnation, human bodies and their physical need became important to us in a whole new way. After Jesus fed the hungry and blessed daily bread, bread that previously had been an economic issue became a spiritual issue.

Plato taught that, in order to be our best, we must be better than our bodies, rising above our decaying, decadent flesh through philosophical contemplation. Incarnational faith believes that while we humans are more than our bodies, we are never less than our bodies. There is no soul apart from the body, no Holy Spirit without the Incarnate Son, no resurrection without the body. If Jesus had not taken on flesh, we would not have known that God is embodied. We would not have known where to look for God in human history. As for us, we are bodies groaning for redemption of our bodies (Rom. 8:22-23).

Paul's favorite term for the church is "Body of Christ." The church is the way the risen Christ continues to take up room in our world and become incarnate to us. Sometimes people in the church complain, "This church is consumed with raising a budget, keeping a roof over our heads, and tinkering with organizational structure when we are supposed to be about more spiritual matters." When we worry about the material form our faith takes, when we work to make our church's structures and organization more effective and fruitful, we *are* being spiritual. Speaking as a pastor, when we pastors concern ourselves with the nuts and bolts of the congregation, when we work for unity and love at St. Luke's On the Interstate, we are being spiritual leaders. We are not free to care for people's disembodied "soul" while ignoring their growling empty stomachs. In the Lord's Prayer, Jesus urges us to pray for material "daily bread" before we pray for spiritual forgiveness or deliverance from temptation.

I am a preacher. I write out my sermons and attempt to make them clear, reasonable, and logical. But I know enough of the incarnational faith to know that the human words that I have written on the page are not a true "sermon." A sermon is faithful only as it is performed, embodied, and made incarnate in the lives of Christians, not as it is spoken by me. Jesus didn't just speak truth to us; he performed truth, enfleshed the word. What is more, he commanded us to do the same. The faith of Christ is not a set of spiritual propositions but rather an embodied, enacted relationship with a crucified Jew who is also "the way" that we are commanded to walk, "the truth" that we are meant to embody, and "the life" that we are meant to live.

Southern writer Flannery O'Connor said, "I am always astonished at the emphasis the Church puts on the body. It is not the soul she [the church] says that will rise but the body, glorified."[1]

Incarnational faith demanded embodiment in architecture and in the visual arts. We should not be surprised by Christianity's artistic impulse. Artists love flesh. It is difficult to think about flesh in the same way after seeing baroque artist Peter Paul Rubens work flesh. Artists honor creation by working with material stuff——paint, stone, wood, and clay—thus adding something beautiful to the world. The art of Michelangelo, Raphael, or Georges Rouault is the expected product of a faith that believes "the Word became flesh."

It's no surprise that a poem is able to speak of Incarnation better than my mere prose. The last two stanzas of "Christmas" by John Betjeman:

> And is it true? For if it is,
> No loving fingers tying strings

Around those tissued fripperies,
The sweet and silly Christmas things,
Bath salts and inexpensive scent
And hideous tie so kindly meant.

No love that in a family dwells,
No carolling in frosty air,
Nor all the steeple-shaking bells
Can with this single Truth compare—
That God was Man in Palestine
And lives today in Bread and Wine.[2]

"God" Is the One Who Speaks and Acts Like Jesus

Christians have been let in on an open secret about God: God was in Jesus Christ reconciling the world. We are not free to make God into anything we please. In Christ a once distant and unknowable God became present and available to us. It is only on the basis of what we know of God in Christ that we are able to say things like, "God is love." Jesus showed us God's love in action—seeking, saving, self-sacrificing, and suffering.

Thus Duns Scotus (c. 1265–1308) said that even if we had not sinned and rebelled against God, necessitating forgiveness and reconciliation by the cross of Christ, God would have still come for us, would still have loved us. God appears determined not to rule aloof and alone in heaven without being surrounded by our presence, love, and praise. God did not simply look down from on high and say, "I love you." God showed up, coming to us as love personified, embodied here, now.

> God appears determined not to rule aloof and alone in heaven without being surrounded by our presence, love, and praise.

Because of the Incarnation we Christians do not attempt to fashion God to suit our inclinations and desires; we pray that our desires and inclinations will be formed by God as revealed by Jesus Christ. Our big question, "Who is God?" has been answered graciously by God. Then we ask, "How ought we live now that we know who God is?"

When former Vice President Cheney defended the use of torture against our country's enemies, a layperson I know called him to task saying, "I'm against torture because that's the way they murdered God's only Son."

At the base of Christian ethics is the Incarnation. We can't let ourselves off the ethical hook by saying, "Jesus forgave his enemies—but of course Jesus was divine and we aren't." No, Jesus exercised forgiveness and nonviolence in this world—our world. His humanness wasn't fake. He forgave his enemies and commanded us to do the same. His way and his words cannot be dismissed as heavenly ideals; they are earthly claims.

The gospel is an announcement (God is with us) and a summons, "Come, be part of this new reality." Because God has incarnated, because the Trinity has thus made the world a stage on which is enacted the drama of our redemption, we are invited to join in God's redemptive work in the world, to tell the whole world the whole truth about God With Us.

"I come here once a week to wash dishes after our breakfast for the homeless, because I feel closer to Christ while serving at this sink than I do sitting in a pew at church." A woman was explaining to me why she offered one morning a week in service at the sink of her congregation's meals for the homeless. Standing there at the sink, explaining her vocation to me, she was for me a living embodiment of Incarnation. When God came to us, God came as a homeless person.

I've seen a sign in some people's gardens that says, "I feel nearer to God in the garden than anywhere else." And I know a lot of people who unashamedly shower affection upon their pets that they would never show to a fellow human being. Gardening is fine and dogs and cats make great companions, but Christians feel near to God when we relate to God the same way God related to us—through humanity.

In Christ, God has made a decision for all time about us: "I will be your God and you will be my people." God's decision, as embodied and exemplified in Christ, challenges us to make our decision: Will we live in light of this world-changing reality or will we appear oddly out of step?

The Truth about God, the Truth about Us

The Incarnation means that Jesus is the whole truth of God. Just as we can't make God mean anything we like, we cannot make God so distant and vague as to be irrelevant. Thus the Incarnation in its ethical substance gives the Christian faith. This is who God is, all the way down. There is no God hiding behind Jesus, as theologian Thomas Torrance loved to say. The church does not define who Jesus is; rather the church is defined by Jesus, who tells us who we are and what we are to be doing.

> The Incarnation means that Jesus is the whole truth of God.

As bishop I received a complaint that one of the pastors under my care had prayed for Osama bin Laden in the Sunday service. Some of the folk in that congregation were incensed. When I called and asked the pastor what he meant in praying for such a vile human being, he replied, "Bishop, I actually believe that the Jew who said, 'Pray for your enemies and bless those who persecute you,' was the Son of God."

Oh, the perils of truly believing that Jesus Christ was fully God and fully human!

Jesus is the truth, the whole truth, and nothing but the truth about God, and also the truth about us. The Incarnation reveals not only the glory of beings stamped in the image of God but also our wretchedness and the perverse ways we have defaced that divine stamp of approval. That's one reason Advent, the season in which we celebrate the Incarnation, is a season of repentance. Very good Jesus brought out the very worst in us. In many of Jesus' parables, the people who presumed to be closest to God through their piety and devotion turned out to be the most mistaken about God. We thought we were fairly good people until we found ourselves at the foot of the cross.

And yet God refused to let our sin, our rebellion and evil, be the end of the story. In Incarnation, God reclaimed us. All this—the enfleshment of God in Christ, Jesus' teachings and deeds, his sacrificial death on the cross, his stunningly unexpected resurrection, and his relentlessly showing up in your church and mine—is "for us and our salvation." Sometimes Christians have respected God so much, lifting God up so high and distant, that their faith morphed into atheism. Because we could not, in our misguided efforts, come to God, God came to us. Our God feels for us and cares about us. God acts, reaches, embraces, risks, saves, and calls. God is close to us, intimate and personally involved. We would have known none of that without Jesus.

The Incarnation also implies that truth is personal, embodied. What is the Christian faith about? It is about Jesus, the one who said, "I am the way, the truth, and the life." We do not worship principles, abstractions, propositions, or an ancient book. We worship the man Jesus. His voice calls to us, seeking out his lost sheep, inviting us to his table. The tears he shed at the death of his friend Lazarus, his homey parables, and above all his cry of dereliction from the cross resonate with us as being truly, deeply human—though hauntingly mysterious at the same time. Here we have fully believable human nature, but also human nature transposed to a different mode of being.

The humility of Christ reveals the divine precisely in its manner of being human. We are most human not in our heroic, Promethean achievements, our vaunted intellect, or our will to power; we are most human in our loving, humble, self-sacrificial service to others in need. Just like Jesus.

We are most human in our loving, humble, self-sacrificial service to others in need. Just like Jesus.

Human life has value, not necessarily because we are inherently valuable, but because God values us. We are loved not because we are lovable but because God is pure, unbounded, active love. Abortion? Capital punishment? War and violent crime? Having seen the extraordinary lengths that God has taken to give and then to redeem human life, we are not free to take what belongs to God. In the Incarnation, God has stood in solidarity with each human life, even the most wretched life in the worst of situations, and shouted for all the world to hear, "Mine!"

Word Made Flesh

In a recent book on the Bible, Professor Bart Erhman asks believers, "Are you willing to put your trust in a thoroughly human, sometimes inaccurate book?"[3] Perhaps because he thinks the Incarnation is hooey, the professor finds it incomprehensible that Christians find God revealed in a thoroughly human book, the Bible.

Having so decisively met God in the thoroughly human Jesus, we learn not to despise the human and to expect God to show up in thoroughly human ways. The Bible is the conjunction of the divine and the human. Scripture is the word of God and the words of people. The Bible didn't fall directly from heaven, anymore than our Lord did. Islam claims that for the Qur'an, but Christians have never made such claims for the Bible because ours is an incarnational faith. The conjunction of the divine and the human is difficult to define, in the Bible or in Jesus. Christians may have some fierce arguments over just what is divine and what is human in Scripture. However each of us knows the delicious mystery of simply reading or hearing Scripture, just following the ordinary human words only to have Scripture reach out to us, take our hand, touch our hearts, and engage us in more than words can say. Let us savor this mystery rather than attempt to define it.

The error of biblical fundamentalism has typically been to identify and specify human words as the word of God. The error of biblical liberalism has been to sharply divide and to contrast human words with divine word. Again, to think like a Christian is to practice conjunctive thinking—Jesus Christ is fully human, fully God. So is God's word.

In words that lie upon a page of Scripture or words spoken by a thoroughly human preacher, sometimes, by the work of God, it becomes the word made flesh. The word is again "fulfilled in your hearing" (Luke 4:21 NRSV). The word dwells in us richly (Col. 3:16), and in spite of all our defenses against speech by a living God, we hear. Thus many of us believe in the truth of Incarnation not because it is church doctrine but because it is a frequent occurrence in our own lives.

Dietrich Bonhoeffer boldly linked preaching with the word made flesh:

> The proclaimed word has its origin in the incarnation of Jesus Christ. It neither originates from a truth once perceived nor from personal experience. . . . The proclaimed word is the incarnate Christ himself . . . the thing itself. The preached Christ is both this Historical One and the Present One. . . . He is the access to the historical Jesus. Therefore the proclaimed word is not a medium of expression for something else, something which lies behind it, but rather it is Christ himself walking through his congregation as the word.[4]

When preaching works, said Bonhoeffer, it is as if the risen Christ walks among his people, speaking to them, commissioning them, calling them with his distinctive "Follow me."

Bonhoeffer's faith in preaching is quite a claim to make for the human words of all-too-human preachers. It is a claim based not upon the alleged gifts of preachers but upon what we know of God in Christ through the Incarnation. It is of the nature of this relentlessly self-revealing God to preach: "In the past, God spoke through the prophets to our ancestors in many times and many ways. In these final days, though, he spoke to us through a Son" (Heb. 1:1-2).

The Incarnation is the great mystery that makes preaching possible. Preaching is a divinely wrought, miraculous act, nothing less than God's speech, God's chosen means of self-revelation. If a sermon "works," it does so as a gracious gift of God, a miracle no less than the virginal conception of Jesus by the Holy Spirit. One reason Christians tend to believe in the likelihood of miracles like the virgin birth of Jesus or the resurrection of Christ is that we have experienced miracles of a similar order, if not similar magnitude, in our own lives as we have listened to a sermon. Something has come to us from afar; something has been born in us that we ourselves did not conceive. A word has been heard that is not self-derived. It's a mysterious, undeserved gift. It's a miracle. Thus preaching is theological not only in its substance but also in its means. Preaching is talk *about* God and miraculous talk *by* God.

At the same time preaching is an utterly human, mundane, carnal, and fleshly thing. Bonhoeffer says, "The proclaimed word is the Christ bearing human nature. This word is . . . the Incarnate One who bears the sins of the world." Aristotle defined a human being as a "word-using animal." For God to speak words to us animals, to become embodied in the words of Scripture or a sermon, requires God to stoop, to take up our nature, and to risk enfleshment. A less secure, less sovereign and free godlet might have kept silent rather than risk intercourse with us on our level. To talk with us is to take up the sins of the world, to risk entanglement in our sinful evasion of the truth. If Christ had not preached to us, presumably we would have had little reason to crucify him. His sermons, in a sense, brought out the worst in us. He told us the truth about God, and we hated him for it. Yet in his resurrection, he resumed the conversation. The talk between us and God is not over until God says it's over: "You surround me—front and back. You put your hand on me. That kind of knowledge is too much for me; it's so high above me that I can't fathom it" (Ps. 139:5-6).

John Chrysostom (c. 347–407), called by his hearers "The Golden Tongued," spoke eloquently and frequently of the Incarnation as God's glorious "condescension" that makes possible our deification. God loves us so much, said Chrysostom, that God came down among us and talked our talk and walked our walk so that we, even in our limited understanding, might know God. God spoke to us in a manner that fit our limitations. Revelation is linked to graciousness. We know about God; we hear God's word only as a gift of a gracious

God. In a wonderful sermon on Genesis 3:8, Chrysostom spoke of the gracious way in which "they heard the sound of the Lord God walking in the garden." Chrysostom said it's a wonderful God who risks all and dares to stroll beside us in the garden, uttering things to us that we can understand; God getting down on our level.

We preachers seek to perform the word in our sermons so that the congregation might enact the word in the world: "You are the body of Christ" (1 Cor. 12:27). We preach in the awesome awareness that the church is, for better or worse, the physical form that the Risen Christ has chosen to take in the world. We preach to the body so that it might be the body of Christ: "Look! I'm standing at the door and knocking. If any hear my voice and open the door, I will come in to be with them, and will have dinner with them, and they will have dinner with me" (Rev. 3:20).

Only Luke's Gospel tells us anything about the childhood of Jesus (e.g., Luke 2:41-52). The one who is God's "Son, the Beloved" (3:22 NRSV) is presented to us as a twelve-year-old who is a learner, a student who is able to grow "with wisdom . . . and in favor with God and with people" (2:40, 52). It may be easier to receive Jesus as a cuddly baby in a manger than as a smart-aleck adolescent! It is also somewhat of a jolt to some of our preconceptions of God to find that Jesus grows, learns, and has ambiguous interactions with his parents. Young

Jesus asks questions but he also answers them (2:46-47). How sad that some Christians (like those who would never take the trouble to read a book on the Incarnation) think they do not need to grow and learn.

Jesus' full humanity is further underscored when he talks back to his distraught parents. Jesus doesn't tell Mary and Joseph that he intends to linger at the temple when the rest of the family heads for home. When his frantic parents find him he responds, "Didn't you know that it was necessary for me to be in my Father's house?" (2:49). It's rather amazing that Luke—so intent on presenting Jesus as the long-expected Messiah, God's Son, Savior of the World—should record this event that presents Jesus as a thoroughly human, though almost insufferably precocious preteen, growing up in a family where there are tensions and conflict. Remind you of any families that you know?

Irenaeus in the second century marveled that God became available to us in Jesus by living through various life stages:

> He came to save all through himself . . . infants, children, boys, young men and old. Therefore he passed through every stage of life: he was made an infant for infants, sanctifying infancy; a child among children, sanctifying those of this age; an example also to them of filial affection . . . a young man amongst young men, an example to them, and sanctifying them to the Lord.[5]

Luke ends the story of Jesus and his parents at the temple by noting that, precocious though Jesus may be, he is still obedient to his parents. Jesus' divinity does not preclude him from respect shown toward his parents. Luke also notes that Mary, even though she seems in this case befuddled by Jesus' words, "treasured all these things in her heart." Jesus is Mary's child, yet even in these early days his perceptive mother knew that he was more than her child. He is marked as favored and as having a unique vocation. His own mother must grow in her comprehension of him.

Take this rare glimpse of the childhood of Jesus in Luke 2 as Luke's brilliant portrayal of the complexities of what we now call Incarnation. God, the one who flung the planets in their courses and set the stars in heaven, comes to us as Jesus, not in some general or universal way, but as a little boy anchored firmly in the faith of Israel and in fulfillment of the promises of God to Israel. He grows under the care of his parents and studies the Scriptures, growing in wisdom and stature, finding favor with some, arousing murderous hostility in others. He is so utterly human, so believably one of us, that we are able closely to identify with him, to recognize our own mundane tensions and conflicts being lived out in him.

At the same time, Jesus Christ is so utterly divine that we do not immediately understand him. We must take time with him, even as through him God has taken time for us. Having apprehended him in the Gospels, we gradually grow in our comprehension of him through the church's worship and through our attempts to follow him in the world. Our wonder at him widens even as we come closer to him. With him, there is always more. His love for us is inexhaustible; his burning desire to have us as his own, unquenchable. This is our only hope.

One of the challenges I faced as dean of Duke University Chapel was Christmas Eve. From one point of view, Christmas Eve was the best time to be at Duke Chapel, with the magnificent Gothic chapel fully decorated, twinkling in candlelight, for three jam-packed evening services. Yet from a preacher's point of view, Christmas Eve at the chapel was almost too much.

"They know not why they are here," I said to myself as I watched people fighting to get in for the first service, acting as if they were at a Black Friday sale and not at a church on Christmas Eve. Ten thousand people from all over the world, some having traveled hours to be there, stood in line for almost as long to get a seat. And then there was the pushing, shoving, and scrambling for seats when the doors opened. There were screaming babies, and people young and old who obviously had not been in a service of Christian worship in a long time.

"We do not allow smoking in the building!" I said to a man lighting a cigar just as a chorister began, "Once in David's Royal City."

Why such throngs? Why such eagerness to get into church for a once-a-year visit? Of course the beauty of the building has something to do with it, and the sentimentality that oozes all around the yuletide. Yes. But such explanations never seemed adequately to explain the phenomenon of Christmas Eve in Duke Chapel.

Here's what I think: though these masses surging in for the Eve of the Nativity may be able to sing along with "O Little Town of Bethlehem," they know next to nothing about Christian theology, certainly nothing of the Christian Doctrine of the Incarnation. But they do know enough to know that here is celebration of good news *that is good news for them.*

Most of the time the church seems aloof from their lives and unaware of their need. The Christian faith appears complicated, judgmental, and arcane. God? A vague, remote enigma. But tonight, when a young lector pronounces, "The Word was made flesh and dwelt among us," they inchoately but deeply understand that this is a word from God to them. The truth about God is that God is for us. Love moves the world, all the way down. Our destiny is communion rather than oblivion. Jesus Christ is God With Us.

And that's why they flock in on Christmas Eve. And that's why they sing and tears come to their eyes, even if they can't fully say why, moved to the depths of their souls by the wonder of Incarnation. Even as Christ

> The truth about God is that God is for us. Love moves the world, all the way down. Our destiny is communion rather than oblivion. Jesus Christ is God With Us.

pursued us, sharing the heights and depths of our full humanity, seeking and searching, finding us in our need, forgiving us the sin for which we could not forgive ourselves, he has given us the means truly to seek and to find him. Having lovingly found us, he then calls us, giving us the grace to follow. Thus Christ's saving work—begun in a cowshed in Bethlehem, manifested in his compassionate signs and wonders, endured through the hell of Golgotha and Calvary, and continued here and now by his glorious resurrection—is brought to consummation. Creation is restored, heaven and earth now mingled in indissoluble union. God With Us so that we might be with God.

This is the most important word Christians have to say to the world. This, the grandeur of Incarnation.

Notes

Chapter 1: God Revealing God

1. Karl Barth, *Credo* (New York: Scribner's, 1962), 68.

2. Søren Kierkegaard, *Philosophical Fragments*, trans. Howard V. Hong and Edna H. Hong (Princeton, NJ: Princeton University Press, 1985), 67.

Chapter 3: Help Is on the Way

1. Stephen Seamands, *Give Them Christ* (Downers Grove, IL: InterVarsity, 2012), 34–35.

2. G. K. Chesterton, *Orthodoxy* (New York: Doubleday, 1959), 92.

3. Ibid., 95.

4. Marcus J. Borg and N. T. Wright, *The Meaning of Jesus: Two Versions* (San Francisco: HarperSanFrancisco, 1999), 146.

5. Ibid., 147–48.

6. Ibid., 168.

7. Philip D. Yancey, *The Jesus I Never Knew* (Grand Rapids: Zondervan, 1995), 28.

Chapter 4: Life in the Light of Incarnation

1. Flannery O'Connor, *The Habit of Being: Letters of Flanner O'Connor* (New York: Farrar, Straus, and Giroux, 1979), 17.

2. John Betjeman, "Christmas," from *A Few Late Chrysanthemums* (London: Murray, 1955).

3. Bart D. Ehrman, *Misquoting Jesus: The Story Behind Who Changed the Bible and Why* (San Francisco: HarperSanFrancisco, 2005), 231.

4. Dietrich Bonhoeffer, *Worldly Preaching*, ed. Clyde E. Fant (Nashville: Thomas Nelson, 1975), 123.

5. Adv. Haer. II.22.4; cited in Bettenson, ed., *Documents of the Christian Church* (Oxford: Oxford University Press, 1963), 30; quoted in Peter K. Stevenson and Stephen Wright, *Preaching the Incarnation*, (Louisville: Westminster John Knox Press, 2010), 64.

CPSIA information can be obtained at www.ICGtesting.com
Printed in the USA
LVOW13s1212050514

384446LV00003B/3/P